IMAGES
of America

LEMONT

Twenty years following Lemont's organization as a village, the cornerstone for a new village hall was set on September 17, 1893. It was eloquently described as "an improvement that will stand for centuries as a monument to the enterprise, intelligence and progressive spirit of the people of the present Lemont." The stone inscription on the front of the building has always read "City Hall." (Courtesy of Lemont Area Historical Society.)

ON THE COVER: A family poses in front of the Fruhauf Building, one of Lemont's most iconic limestone structures. Since its construction in 1871 at 107 Stephen Street, this building has stood as a tavern and is now a restaurant. It has also been known as Emil Wend's Tavern, Tom's Place (its first home), the Silver Jug, the Christmas Tree Inn, and for the past 30-plus years, La Dolce Vita. The arched cornice bearing the name Charles Fruhauf has become a symbol of downtown Lemont, and was included in the winning design for Lemont's 150th anniversary logo. (Courtesy of Lemont Area Historical Society.)

IMAGES
of America

LEMONT

Kevin Barron and Jason Berry in association
with the Lemont Area Historical Society
Foreword by Pat Camalliere

ARCADIA
PUBLISHING

Published by Arcadia Publishing
Charleston, South Carolina

Printed in the United States of America

Library of Congress Control Number: 2023937940

For all general information, please contact Arcadia Publishing:
Telephone 843-853-2070
Fax 843-853-0044
E-mail sales@arcadiapublishing.com

Visit us on the Internet at www.arcadiapublishing.com

Kevin: to friends, family, and neighbors in Lemont.
Jason: to Mary, forever ready to guide and support, with love.

CONTENTS

ACKNOWLEDGMENTS

Since its founding, the Lemont Area Historical Society (LAHS) and Museum has been dedicated to protecting, celebrating, and growing Lemont's history. It has taken a leading role to preserve the community's significant buildings and landscapes and joins in events that bring Lemonters together. It is impossible to individually thank all the boards, members, and volunteers throughout the years, nor the thousands who have visited the museum or attended society programs and tours. Together, all have helped ensure that the LAHS continues to collect and maintain the community's many treasured memories while offering programs that keep a vibrant history alive in the present and for our future.

A special thank-you goes to Pat Camalliere, who more than anyone was dedicated to helping us tell a good story, tell the right story, and make sure it is something you will enjoy reading as much as we know you will enjoy the images. Pat's influence is on every page of this book. Also, thanks go to Susan Donahue, Barb Bannon, Gail August, and Tricia O'Neill for answering our questions and sharing their knowledge. We thank John Quinn for his efforts to digitize the LAHS collection, which provided our first look at the archives. Abigail Rose from All Together Studio created our custom maps—thank you. And we are grateful for Barbara Buschman, editor of two histories of Lemont, the centennial book and the 125th anniversary edition. Without these volumes, ours would not have been possible. All those who worked on these books were an inspiration. At the Village of Lemont, George Schafer and Linda Molitor have our gratitude for their support.

In 2023, the board of the Lemont Area Historical Society includes Susan Donahue, president; Traci Sarpalius, vice president No. 1; Two Carol Garibay, vice president No. 2; Terry Blanz, treasurer; Sue Roy, secretary; and board members Jason Berry, Charmaine Drafke, Patricia Knight, Tricia O'Neill, John Quinn, Jason Smith, and Jackie Uzanski, supported by committee members Gail August, Barb Bannon, Diane Butkovich, Pat Camalliere, Tim Collins, and tour guides Kevin Barron, Doris Peterman, Paul Pfeifer.

Unless otherwise noted, all images are from the archives of the Lemont Area Historical Society and Museum.

FOREWORD

When I moved to Lemont 25 years ago, I was told, "You'll never be a 'True Lemonter.' You haven't been here your whole life." Those words did not stop me from almost immediately falling under a spell that sparked a passion for my adopted town, which has only increased through the years.

That passion led me to volunteer for the Lemont Area Historical Society, where I now manage the society's archives. As I learned more of the fascinating, important, and quirky history of Lemont, I was inspired to write novels that focus on Lemont's history. I hoped through stories to gift my enthusiasm for my adopted town to others.

For Lemont is like no other place. It is set apart from the suburban sprawl, occupying the hills, bluff, and mile-wide valley of the Des Plaines River, surrounded in large part by forests and farms, tucked between picturesque hills and ravines, with a small-town flavor that calms one's soul. We who live here can step away from our hectic world, as if every day were a vacation.

Yet for all that, you will learn Lemont's importance in the early history of this country, its part in paving the way to opening the continent to settlement, the canal that made possible transportation from sea to sea and the growth of Chicago.

Jason Berry and Kevin Barron, like me, are not natives of Lemont, but I understand what led them to take on the challenge of writing this book, since we share the experience of falling in love with this town. This book was conceived and grew from a desire to share our affection as Lemont reaches its 150th anniversary. Having been part of their process, I believe no one else could tell Lemont's story as well.

And so we maintain, we are "True Lemonters." Whether you have indeed lived your whole life in Lemont or if you know nothing at all about our town, we invite you to learn on these pages to treasure Lemont the way we do.

Pat Camalliere
Archivist, Lemont Area Historical Society
Author, The Cora Tozzi Historical Mystery Series

INTRODUCTION

Our village was destined to be Lemont. From the banks of La Rivière des Plaines, lined thick with trees, a mount rose on bluffs over bedrock in magnificent contrast to the flat prairie grasslands of Illinois. Early French explorers, led by Native American guides, were so impressed that they chose this place as the site of a passage from the Great Lakes to the Mississippi River.

It is seen on early maps as Palmyra, the first name for Lemont Township. It is not known where that name came from, or who suggested Lemont. But on April 2, 1850, at the home of Lemuel Brown, the Town of Lemont was chosen. Its population had grown to over 3,000 inhabitants. Still earlier names from "paper towns"—recorded on plats to sell real estate to speculation-minded buyers—can be found: Keepotaw (today's Keepataw) and Athens side-by-side with Lemont. On June 9, 1873, the town voted unanimously to incorporate as the Village of Lemont. A century later, Lemont's population numbered only 5,500. Over the next 50 years, the community would witness unprecedented growth.

This is a book of Lemont's history, but not a history book. There has always been a collection of Lemont images, principally through the archives of the Lemont Area Historical Society. Our goal was to showcase this collection and publish a book to coincide with the 150th anniversary of Lemont's incorporation as a village, along with numerous other anniversaries happening in 2023. While not a complete history of Lemont, this is a look into Lemont's story through the archives of the LAHS and the donations of its board, membership, and the Lemont community. These are just a few of the thousands of photographs, postcards, books, maps, records, and copious ephemera and publications in the library, not to mention the historical museum that exhibits objects and artifacts preserved by the historical society. By focusing on the society's collection, we acknowledge all those who built this tremendous organization.

The book begins with Lemont's founding and continues with the incredible and transformative twins of the quarry industry and the Chicago Sanitary and Ship Canal, as it is known today; Lemont's shadowy industry of Smokey Row; early public institutions including the formation of the Village of Lemont, school districts, and the arrival of other religious institutions; and the industrial revolutions, the bridges, buildings, and businesses that made up Lemont early in the 20th century.

The story takes us up to the 1970s, when Lemont celebrated its first centennial and the historical society was formed, and a bit beyond to include some significant events. There are many more stories we did not have space to share, but we look forward to presenting them in the future. If you do not see yourself or your organization in this book, it was not because you were forgotten. Any omissions—and we acknowledge there are some notable ones—were because the material was not found in the LAHS archives. We encourage everyone to consider helping this archive grow. If we are fortunate, there may be future volumes.

One

ANCIENT LANDSCAPES

Lemont was born from forces greater than human intervention. The advance and retreat of glaciers and the outflows of an ancient lake formed moraines and exposed bedrock along the Des Plaines River, meeting in Lemont and creating the broad wetlands of the Sag Valley. During the ice age some 70,000 years ago, early Lake Michigan (Lake Chicago) was held in place by the Wisconsin glacier to the north and the Des Plaines River outlet. When a second outlet to the south topped the moraines near Lemont, meltwater flowed toward the Des Plaines River. As Lake Chicago drained through these gaps, Mount Forest Island was formed, and the waters eroded the Des Plaines River valley in Lemont down to bedrock in places. This set the stage for incredible industrial advancements in the 19th century, beginning with the Illinois and Michigan Canal and Lemont's quarrying industry.

The 1816 Treaty of St. Louis ceded a strip of Native American land 20 miles wide from the mouth of the Chicago River west to the Illinois River. This territory appeared on maps as the Indian Boundary Line, dividing federal and Native lands in the old Northwest. Within these borders, plans were made for a canal, achieving the vision of French missionary Fr. Jacques Marquette and explorer Louis Jolliet from 1673. By agreement in the Treaty of Chicago in 1833, the local Potawatomi Nation and all other tribes would leave their Illinois lands. The Northwest was now open for settlement, and the proposed canal would provide transportation routes from coast to coast.

Canal workers—Irish immigrants mostly, having experience building the Erie Canal—began arriving in Lemont in the 1830s to build the I&M Canal. Lemont's first Yankee and European residents were farmers, preferring the flat agricultural lands on the top of the river bluff, south of the present-day downtown. The canal would soon take prominence in Lemont life, becoming the most important trade route in the United States and ensuring Chicago's prominence as a commercial center.

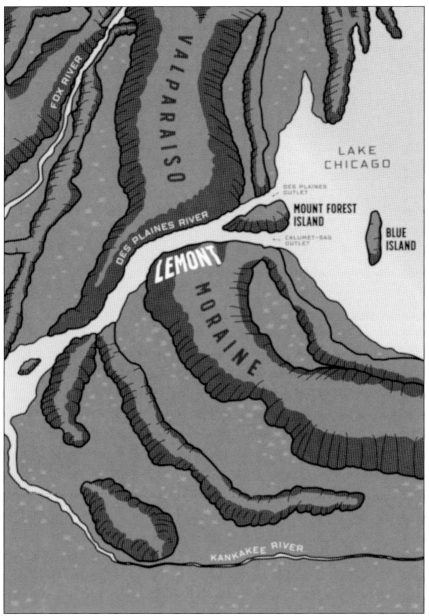

The area that is now Lemont was formed by the movement of glaciers that left behind a landscape of rolling hills and valleys. Lake Chicago, as early Lake Michigan is called, emptied through breaks in moraines that circled its southwest border, today's confluence of the Chicago Sanitary and Ship Canal and the Calumet-Saganashkee (Cal-Sag) Channel. From the perch of Mount Forest Island, where St. James at Sag Bridge stands, one can trace these spillways where the two canals were built following the low ground and gaps created as the Wisconsin glacier melted. Erosion from the retreat of the glacier and lake exposed bedrock. This magnesium-rich stone, called dolomite, was formed in the reefs of the Silurian Sea over 400 million years ago. The moraines that border Lemont, with the river and valleys, created a verdant green band, which explains why Lemont today is known for its rivers, trails, hiking, and hills. This terrain was ideal for early human habitation, and centuries later was likely visited by French missionaries, explorers, and traders.

Looking east from Sag Bridge, the old Calumet Feeder Canal cuts through Saganashkee Slough. This ancient landscape is identified by Mount Forest Island to the north and the glacial till left by the Tinley and Valparaiso moraines to the south. Near here, a melting glacial stream left behind the only exposed dolomite canyon in Cook County. (Courtesy of the Metropolitan Water Reclamation District of Greater Chicago.)

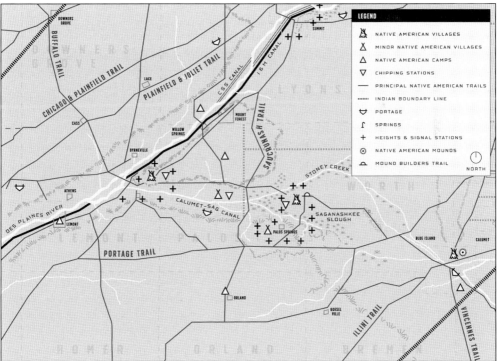

The Council of the Three Fires, consisting of the Potawatomi, Odawa, and Ojibwe, were the major Native tribes to confront a growing United States in the area. Lemont's rivers and high moraines had provided an excellent site for indigenous villages, with abundant hunting and fishing, and trails for transportation and trade. Albert F. Scharf, charting a lost landscape, made this map of their trails and villages from the 1800s.

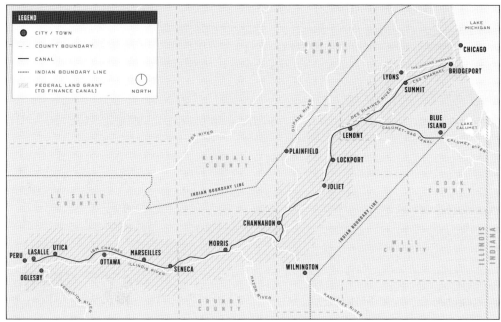

The 1816 Treaty of St. Louis created an Indian Boundary Line. The boundary was drawn 10 miles on each side of a line from the mouth of the Chicago River at Lake Michigan west to the Illinois River, destined to connect markets from the Great Lakes westward. Federal lands were granted to the state and sold to finance the Illinois and Michigan Canal, which opened in 1848.

The *Lemont Press*, describing the town of the 1830s, wrote that "Lemont was at that time a very haven of rest, a fit study for the artist. Then nature could be seen in all her beauty . . . its beautiful hill, one dense forest, untenanted save by the birds and wild game; the deer, the true monarch of the woods, that came in herds to drink at the river edge."

The first settlers in Lemont Township—then known as Palmyra—preferred the flat, high ground south of the of the river valley. Gathered three miles southeast of today's downtown Lemont, they plowed prairies as broad as the horizon into fields for agriculture and livestock. The names of these early farmers, such as Derby and Bell, live on with local street names that mark their old lands.

The canal builders followed just a few years after the first Yankee landowners and were ready to dig the Illinois and Michigan Canal. Housing for laborers was a primitive mix of log cabin and stones. The completion of the canal led to increased travel, trade, and the development of a new mining industry. The I&M Canal was the artery responsible for the growth of Chicago and Illinois.

During the excavation of the Chicago Drainage Canal, now known as the Chicago Sanitary and Ship Canal, in 1890, relics of Lemont were unearthed. This area was known for its abundance of fossils, particularly those from the Ordovician period (485–443 million years ago). Preserved in the sedimentary rocks of the region, which were covered by the shallow Silurian Sea, it was not surprising to find fossil impressions of sea creatures. This collection displays some of the most common fossils found in Lemont, such as trilobites, shelled cephalopods, crinoids, and corals. Teeth from ice age species could be uncovered in the shallow glacial till. The natural outcroppings of stone here made Lemont an excellent place for Native Americans to craft tools. Numerous arrowheads and stone tools have been found. The notched tools in the foreground are likely hammers. Interesting pieces of stone and old bones were also collected. (Courtesy of the Metropolitan Water Reclamation District of Greater Chicago.)

Two

DYNAMITE AND DOLOMITE

Lemont's earliest industry, the source of its fame and early commercial growth, lies in its geological creation. It is a past so deep that it must be pulled from the earth as stone. The Illinois and Michigan Canal cuts through the Des Plaines River valley in Lemont, following the course of this ancient outlet. When digging the I&M Canal through Lemont, bedrock and dolomite limestone, suitable for building, were discovered near the surface. This discovery led to the establishment of many quarries in Lemont and the birth of an important industry.

Lemont became a quarry town, with the largest quarries employing 400 hardworking men, using the ingenious technology that helped them mine tons of stone annually. Early quarry owners benefited from the experience and technology gathered while building the canal and brought new innovations to the stone business. They found their fortunes in the dolomite limestone that Chicago's capitalists marketed as "Athens marble." Blocks of the yellow-hued dimensional stone, flagstone, and crushed stone were barged to the city. The celebrated historian of Chicago, A.T. Andreas, reported its first use as early as 1852: "The reputation of the Athens stone extended until it became the favorite building material in the city." Chicago's famous Water Tower, built from Lemont limestone, became the surviving symbol of the Great Fire of 1871. The stone ages with a soft, mellow grace now synonymous with the renowned churches of post-fire Chicago such as Holy Name Cathedral, and more proudly so in the many churches and commercial buildings of Lemont.

In the 1870s, Lemont's Singer and Talcott Stone Company grew to be one of the largest of its era, with holdings of 800 acres of quarries. By the time of the construction of the Sanitary District of Chicago's drainage canal, built in the 1890s to reverse the flow of the Chicago River, Lemont's quarries were at a crossroads. The demand for Lemont Limestone was waning in popularity. Labor conditions and violence in the quarries made things difficult for workers and owners alike. Production in Lemont shifted to crushed stone, used in concrete, roadbuilding, and by the railroads.

Drainage Canal. Lemont, Ills. 160 feet wide. 33 feet deep

The "Rock Section" of the Chicago Drainage Canal stretched through Lemont from Willow Springs to Lockport. Dignitaries gathered near Lemont at the border of Cook and Will Counties on September 3, 1892, for Shovel Day, celebrating the construction of the canal by turning dirt and blasting rock. They returned to the spot in 1895 for Tablet Day and set a granite marker in the canal wall.

Lemont, Ill.   5547 Blasting Stone in Drainage Canal

Blasting limestone with dynamite was a typical method in the creation of the Chicago Drainage Canal. Due to the unique geological makeup of the Lemont area, canal-digging was challenging, and explosives were frequently required. An early resident of Lemont reported that he was paid 50¢ a day as a boy to carry blasting equipment and load drilled holes.

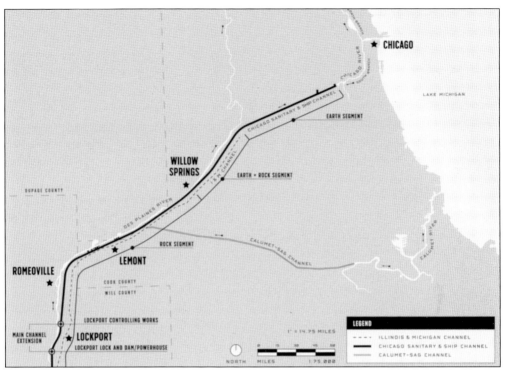

The full length of the Chicago Sanitary and Ship Canal spans 28 miles from the South Branch of the Chicago River to Lockport. The route was selected in 1892, and contracts were awarded by sections. Mason, Hoge, King and Company were the contractors in Lemont, Section No. 8. Each contractor brought their own innovations to the project. The Cal-Sag Channel, shown here, was not completed until 1922.

Lemont's rock made it one of the toughest sections to dig. A channeling machine was used to cut a vertical trench into the rock face as deep as 16 feet. Once a channel was cut, dynamite would be used to explode the rock, which was then moved to piles along the canal banks.

Canal workers are seen drilling holes in the rock surface in 1894. The holes were then packed with dynamite. Other workers load the rubble into cars that travel up an incline, dumping the spoils along the bank. The cuts of the channeling machine are visible on the bedrock wall, the first pass for Section No. 8.

Looking west from Lemont Road, this photograph of construction was taken in the summer of 1894. The cableway system shown here was erected to remove the blasted rock. Hoppers were attached to a wheeled trolley that traveled on the cable between the towers, and the stone spoil was dumped on the canal banks.

Workers in 1895 follow the channeling machine to deepen the canal. A first pass was excavated, then deepened by the machine with a second. Third, the workers cut. A hoist loaded from the canal floor replaced the incline tracks. Quarried stone blocks were set on top of the canal walls using traditional masonry techniques. The Santa Fe Railroad tracks are in the background.

Construction of the canal was a source of pride, fascination, and entertainment. Here, Lemont's Wagner Livery brings a group of tourists to the canal in the winter of 1895–1896 in a horse-drawn sleigh. While quarry operations would stop from November to April, work on the canal continued year-round. The powerhouse for drilling rock and a channeling machine are working in the background.

Copyright, 1895.
Jno. F. Geiger.

95 feet above ground

Some took their visit to the canal to new heights. In 1895, as the canal was nearing completion in Lemont, this group of dignitaries—and someone's dog!—were hoisted 95 feet above ground, with the Chicago Drainage Canal below them and the Des Plaines River valley sprawling behind, in a rural landscape yet untouched by industry. In the back row on the right in the hopper bucket is Lemont's village president John McCarthy. The machinery and manpower required to build the canal was unlike anything the nation had seen. According to Richard Lanyon, visitors to Chicago for the 1893 World's Columbian Exposition toured the construction. The canal was named "The Seventh Wonder of America" by the American Society of Civil Engineers.

Pictured here is 4,450 pounds of dynamite being stored for canal construction, used to blast through bedrock along the 14-mile rock section between Willow Springs and Lockport. This much dynamite could obviously cause some harm. Later, when the Cal-Sag Channel was being built, dynamite blasts damaged nearby St. James at Sag Bridge, requiring stone buttresses on the exterior. (Courtesy of the Metropolitan Water Reclamation District of Greater Chicago.)

Water slowly began to fill the canal as construction completed. On January 2, 1900, the Sanitary District of Chicago commissioners abruptly opened a dam along the Chicago River, releasing water into the Chicago Drainage Canal. In Lemont, last to be built were the bridges that would cross the canal and river. Rock left under the Santa Fe Railroad Bridge completed the excavation.

Drainage Canal at Lemont, Ill.   Loading boats with building stone

The total cost for the section of canal through the village was $1,025,622.87, according to the Sanitary District of Chicago. The stone spoils created by canal excavations were used for construction and expansion of the quarrying industry. Operators could now quickly load rock onto barges to new destinations due to the proximity of crushed stone.

The massive spoil piles on both sides of the Chicago Sanitary and Ship Canal in Lemont became an opportunity for a new industry. American Crushed Stone Company was awarded a contract with the Sanitary District of Chicago for 100,000 cubic yards of rubble in Lemont on the south bank of the canal near Stephen Street, at a cost of 10¢ per cubic yard.

Steam derricks for handling stone and steam canal boats were an innovation first brought to the quarrying industry by Lemont resident Horace M. Singer, of Singer and Talcott Stone Company. The company introduced steam canal boats to the Illinois and Michigan Canal, where they were used to transport Athens marble to Chicago. Steam-powered barges such as the *Martin Hogan* were a common sight later on the Chicago Drainage Canal.

The *Terror's* crew load boxes of stone on the banks of the canal, as the Illinois Stone Company crushing plant works in the distance. The plant could produce various sizes of crushed stone, as the tall house held multiple screens through which the stone could be graded.

Illinois Stone Company, seen in operation here, organized in 1858 and employed approximately 200 workers. Illinois Stone specialized in crushed stone after the demand for dimensional stone—Lemont's celebrated Athens marble—declined in the 1890s. Lemont's quarries remained active by supplying crushed stone for concrete construction, as well as railroad ballast, roads, and agricultural lime.

Illinois Stone Company was later known as Consumers Company. The large quarry at the entrance to Lemont's Heritage Quarries Recreation Area bears its name today. Its holdings were on both sides of the Illinois and Michigan Canal. In 1925, Limestone Resources of Illinois reported a daily production of 1,500 tons and annual production of 400,000 tons per season.

Quarrymen pose at Consumers Company with a Bucyrus 95–C, the largest steam shovel available in its day. A railcar is positioned nearby to transport the crushed rock to boats waiting along the main channel. Bucyrus 95–C shovels were used in rock quarries throughout Illinois and were sent to dig the Panama Canal in the early 1900s.

Great Lakes Dredge and Dock company is loading a dump scow from a massive pile of stone spoil in Lemont. This stone was used by the company for harbor work, with contracts in Gary, Indiana; South Chicago; Wilmette; and North Chicago. Great Lakes Dredge and Dock operated approximately 1.25 miles east of Lemont's downtown district.

Many of the improvements developed while building the Chicago Sanitary and Ship Canal informed the practices of Lemont's quarry owners. Crushed stone is being hand-loaded onto cars on tracks, while a channeling machine is working at left. Like with the construction of the canal, drills and dynamite were still used, although pry bars were the preferred tool in quarrying dimensional stone.

Western Stone Company, seen here working Quarry No. 1, emerged from a consolidation of Lemont's many quarry owners. Western Stone operated five quarries in the Lemont area. Quarry No. 1 is now part of Lemont's Heritage Quarries Recreation Area, the large quarry farthest east in the park. It is known today as Great Lakes Quarry.

The Lemont Limestone Company was west of Lemont Road on the north side of the Chicago Sanitary and Ship Canal. Quarries here were first discovered by Nathaniel J. Brown, a canal contractor who in 1837 excavated a mile of canal in present-day Lemont. In the 1840s, he opened the first quarries in Lemont, which he leased to builders.

Quarries Operating Company mined limestone west of downtown Lemont near the Des Plaines River. The broad Des Plaines River valley, surprisingly picturesque, stretches out behind the company. Nature and industry remain intertwined here, as these quarries along Bluff Road, later abandoned by the Western Stone Company, are now protected habitats managed by the Cook County and Will County Forest Preserve Districts.

The construction of the Chicago Drainage Canal first required re-routing the Des Plaines River. This bridge traversed the diversion, replacing an earlier fixed-timber truss-and-beam bridge. A concrete closed-spandrel arch design, it is said to have been designed by Harry L. Emerson. The bridge was ornamented with rosettes and upright lions with fluted columns for the lights. Heading into Lemont, the Stephen Street Bridge is to the right.

Large limestone blocks and machinery sit idle at one of Western Stone Company's Lemont quarries, very likely the former Great Lakes quarry. Lemont's quarries were worked for eight months, from April through November. It is not uncommon to find photographs of visitors posing among the rocks, shovels, and carts used in quarry operations.

After closing, reportedly the pumps that kept the quarries dry for mining purposes were removed, and the vast industrial landscape found a new purpose: recreation. Here, a large camp is set up at one of the former quarries, with paddle in hand ready to enjoy the day. Fishing at the quarries became a popular pastime. Today, these quarries remain stocked by the Illinois Department of Natural Resources.

In addition to the camps, small game hunting was a popular pastime throughout the Saganashkee Valley. These log cabin huts were used by hunters but were claimed to have been built by some of the Sag's earliest settlers: the Irish immigrants who traveled to Lemont to dig the Illinois and Michigan Canal.

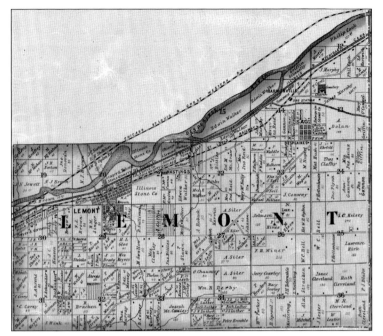

Edwin Walker operated three quarries in Lemont along the I&M Canal, with sawing, planing, and lime kilns. Lemont limestone from Walker's quarries was used to build the Chicago Water Tower and portions of the state capitol. Nearly all of the land in the Heritage Quarries recreation area, with the exception of the quarries owned by the Illinois Stone Company and later Consumers, was once held by the Walkers.

Walker moved his family to Lemont in the late 1860s. His mansion, named Woodland Park, featured bold use of Athens marble and fine wood-carved details. Located near the corner of present-day Walker Road and Main Street, the family's mansion was later used by Our Lady of Victory as a convent. After tornado damage in 1991, the building was torn down for Franciscan Village.

Quarrymen and their families gather in Lemont in 1893 for another strike, the first since 1885. Lemont played a significant role in labor history. In 1885, quarry workers fought to raise the standard wage of $1.50 a day. After clashes in Joliet, the Quarry Owners Association appealed to the state militia. Gov. Richard Oglesby ordered troops to Lemont on May 4, 1885. Three workers were killed, and many were injured.

In 1893, quarry owners pitted canal workers against the miners by dropping wages for unskilled labor. On June 9, quarry workers marching west from Lemont were met by armed guards firing on the strikers. County sheriffs called for the militia. Sent to Lemont by Gov. John Peter Altgeld, the troops were positioned at the Chicago & Alton Railroad tracks. Fearing more violence, Altgeld would later order them to station outside of town.

When Governor Altgeld arrived via train on the Chicago & Alton (depot at left), a crowd of workers, angry about the attempt at military control, had gathered at the village park on Main Street. There, strikers had laid the body of one of the murdered men, Gregor Kisha. Altgeld spoke to the crowd in English and German, assuring them troops would not act. The governor took testimony and interviews from Lemont mayor McCarthy's office. He learned that authorities from the sheriff's offices had lied about rioting in Lemont. A meeting with quarry workers was held with a committee representing Polish, German, Irish, Swedish, and Danish workers. After Governor Altgeld's intervention, workers received the $1.75 daily wage. They returned to work on June 13, 1893. Following Altgeld's visit to Lemont, he pardoned the remaining Haymarket prisoners who led the May 1, 1886, march for the eight-hour workday.

Three

THE SEVEN STEEPLES

Going south on Lemont Road approaching the valley at the foot of downtown Lemont, travelers are greeted by an awe-inspiring landscape on the opposite side of the bluff dotted with the steeples and spires of churches lofting above leafy trees and rooftops. The "Seven Steeples" of the historic early ethnic churches of Lemont played a pivotal role in the religious life and settlement of the community that continues to thrive today. Immigrants brought their languages, traditions, and religious practices from their homelands. Lemont's early religious establishments included a log cabin at State and Main Streets shared by Irish, German, and Polish Catholics. Between the 1850s and 1890s, congregations donated or purchased limestone to build the landmark centers of worship still standing today. Though masonry in Lemont is characterized by local limestone, the churches rebuilt in the 1920s generally followed current regional preferences for brick. Today, five limestone churches and two brick structures make up the original Seven Steeples of Lemont.

Lemont's important location in the Des Plaines River valley ensures an elevated view of its religious institutions, historic and modern. These historic churches closely mirror the communities they are a part of. St. James at Sag Bridge, not only Lemont's oldest limestone church but one of the oldest churches in northeastern Illinois, traces its past to prehistoric Mount Forest Island. Lemont's Swedish community established Bethany Lutheran. German residents founded Lutheran and Catholic congregations. Lemont Methodist Episcopal, once known for its temperance crusades and moral activism, is now home to the Lemont Area Historical Society and Museum. SS. Cyril and Methodius, which boasted that its steeple was the highest point in Cook County, is built on a square in Jasnagora, Lemont's first Polish neighborhood .

Whether approaching on a canal boat through the valley, in a streetcar along New Avenue, or an automobile across the Stephen Street Bridge, Lemont's steeples have welcomed residents and visitors for over a century, not only as architectural gems but as religious institutions serving generations.

Picturesque Lemont, with its storied church steeples and spires built into the southern bluff of the Des Plaines River valley, has always left an impression on visitors as well as residents. The steeples of SS. Cyril and Methodius (left) and Bethany Lutheran (right) frame this bucolic scene of early Lemont and its rolling landscape.

From the top of Lemont Street looking north, Bethany Lutheran can be seen on the left and the two steeples in the distance are Lemont Methodist Episcopal (left), and St. Matthew Evangelical Lutheran. Lemont's rural roots are represented by a horse and buggy. The home to the left of Bethany Lutheran no longer stands, but would have sat between the current church and its original location.

Lemont's earliest church is St. James at Sag Valley, surrounded by an even earlier Catholic cemetery. Begun as a mission station for Irish canal workers, the church was built of limestone beginning in 1853. It is on the edge of Mount Forest Island, an 85-foot-tall bluff carved above the valleys of the Des Plaines River and the Sag.

The oldest Catholic cemetery in Cook County, with burials recorded as early as 1837, speaks to the Irish settlement here. Locally carved marble tombstones reveal the county and parish where the departed were born. The oldest legible marker is for Michael Dillon, from April 26, 1846. Stone for the church was hauled from Roughnot's quarry in Sag Valley by Irish laborers in exchange for the best cemetery plots.

Donated photographs in the 1983 *Sesquicentennial Jubilee Cookbook* reveal the appearance of St. James as many Irish settlers would have known it following its six-year construction starting in 1853 until sometime in the 1880s. Parishioner Dorothy Claffy's notes say this photograph was taken around 1884, before the addition of a permanent roof and limestone steeple. (Courtesy of Father Koys, St. James at Sag Valley.)

Saginaw Hall contains the joists, beams, and hardwood floor of its predecessor, seen here sometime before its 1912 demolition. Church parishioners required a more permanent space to replace the previous Monk's Hall, and the building created with these reused materials still stands at St. James at Sag Bridge property today. (Courtesy of Father Koys, St. James at Sag Valley.)

Lemont Methodist Episcopal Church at 306 Lemont Street is the oldest religious building inside village limits and served its congregation until 1970. The cornerstone was laid on September 14, 1861, and the church opened for services that November. It was built from stone tailings donated from Nathaniel Brown's quarries. Its rustic rubble walls contrast with the strong quoining and dressed stone entrance.

Stained-glass windows at the Methodist Episcopal church were installed in 1892, adding color to the sparse space. They capture the prominence of the church at the time, with the family names of Brown and Singer—both quarry barons—and Norton—prominent merchant trader—among those memorialized. The embossed metal ceiling is from 1924 and was made by the Friedley-Voshardt Company. (Courtesy of Molly Hebda Photography.)

The Methodist congregation has been active in village life. The church building served as a recruiting station during the Civil War. In the 1890s, Reverend Clancy preached against the vice and corruption of Lemont's Smokey Row. Presently known as the Old Stone Church and home to the Lemont Area Historical Society and Museum, the building was listed in the National Register of Historic Places in 1986.

Like Bethany Lutheran, seen here, Lemont's many early churches were built into the hilly bluff of Lemont's historic residential district. They towered over the landscape of their day, a reminder of their importance in the everyday life of Lemont's ethnic enclaves. Lemont churches, historic to modern, were built overlooking hills and valleys.

Bethany Lutheran, a block south of two other 19th-century limestone churches, was known as the Swedish Church. Often, congregations either outgrew or lost their original wood-frame churches to fire. In this rare postcard view, the original 1873 Swedish Evangelical Lutheran Church is still next door (left) to the 1895-built limestone masterpiece where the congregation continues to worship.

Svenska Evangeliska Lutherska Bethania organized on September 22, 1872. The Swedish immigrants taught the Swedish language in their parochial school. As the congregation grew, they needed a larger church. The current structure reflects the congregation's taste for elaborate woodworking and limestone masonry. This photograph donated by the Erickson family shows the interior of Bethany Lutheran around 1900.

Germans were among the earliest to settle in Lemont, and St. Matthew Evangelical Lutheran Church reflects their history. The cornerstone features two dates—the original construction in 1887 and the rebuilt year of 1918, after St. Matthew suffered a severe fire and loss of records. The modest Gothic Revival style features rusticated Lemont limestone throughout and a central square bell tower.

This photograph from 1896 shows the original altar inside St. Matthew before the fire 22 years later. In January 1918, a furnace overheated, resulting in destruction of the entire interior of the church. Although the towering spire was not rebuilt, the original walls—nearly three feet thick—remained, allowing the congregation to rebuild without significant exterior changes.

A St. Matthew Evangelical Lutheran *schule* class poses on the steps in 1903. Classes were held in the building constructed in 1870 by Horace M. Singer as a private subscription school on Illinois Street. Organized as Evangelical Lutheran Mataeus Congregation, the school was purchased from Singer in 1874, which St. Matthew then converted to its first church.

Here is a unique view of St. Matthew Evangelical Lutheran after the 1918 fire, but before 1972. The original German Lutheran church and school is still standing east of the limestone church (left). This school was eventually demolished for the current gymnasium facing Illinois Street. Lemont's elevation, which helps give each church such prominence, is apparent in this view.

St. Alphonsus was founded for Lemont's German Catholics in the 1860s. Their first church can be seen in this view, which stood between 1867 and 1921 nearer to the corner of Custer and State Streets, just north of the current church. As Lemont's Catholic population grew from their shared log cabin church on State and Main Streets, Irish, German, and Polish residents each formed their own parishes.

The cornerstone of the present St. Alphonsus was laid on July 4, 1920. According to the church archives, architect Charles E. Wallace of Joliet was the designer, and local families donated their skilled labor. The stone cross installed on the church remains near the corner of State and Custer Streets with a German inscription that translates to, "He who perseveres to the end will be saved."

The altar at St. Alphonsus is seen before the Second Vatican Council, when the priest would face the altar with his back to the congregation during Mass and only the altar boys accompanied him past the altar rail. While unidentified, these boys were likely German, and congregants may have followed the Mass with a bilingual missal in Latin and German.

Here is a combined gathering of St. Alphonsus and SS. Cyril and Methodius, organized by the Knights of Columbus, in front of St. Alphonsus. Early Catholic immigrants of all ethnic groups originally held Mass together at the first St. Patrick's mission church. The German and Polish communities later organized separate parishes to worship in their own languages and traditions.

Fr. Leopold B.M. Moczygemba, who was serving as the pastor of St. Alphonsus, was commissioned to organize a new parish to serve Lemont's Polish community, to be called SS. Cyril and Methodius. The church and school were completed in 1884, with the first Mass said by Father Moczygemba on Palm Sunday. The frame church stood nearly 120 feet tall. Next to it is a bell tower.

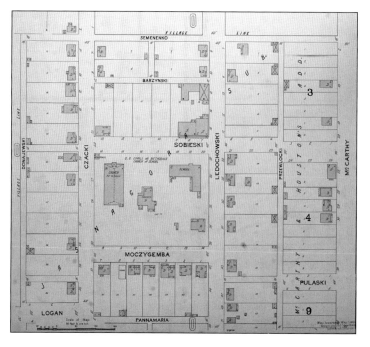

Father Moczygemba purchased 10 acres south and east of the village limits for the congregation in 1883. Land was subdivided as Jasnagora, in honor of the Polish pilgrimage site, and was platted with lots for sale to parishioners, reserving a central square for church buildings. This map shows the arrangement of all wood structures, with a church, parsonage, school, and shops. (Courtesy of Library of Congress.)

SS. Cyril and Methodius's first wood-frame parsonage stood directly in the middle of the central square that Father Moczygemba had laid out for the parish, east of the original frame church. Although the people are unidentified, the steep hill behind the parsonage is unmistakable. This area of Lemont is popularly known as "Blue Hill."

A large crowd gathers for the cornerstone dedication for a new church on April 21, 1929. A devastating fire destroyed the first SS. Cyril and Methodius in the early morning hours on Ash Wednesday in 1928, burning the structure to its foundation. The dedication day was attended by hundreds of parishioners, the Knights of Columbus, and Lemont's Polish organizations.

The new (and current) church and rectory for SS. Cyril and Methodius was designed by architects Brielmaier and Sons of Milwaukee, according to church records. The rectory was completed in 1929, and the first Mass was held on New Year's Day 1930. A shrine to Our Lady of Częstochowa, protector of Poland who saved Jasna Góra during an invasion, is inside.

Plans for the new church were rejected by the cardinal as too large and expensive. Parishioners defied him and built according to the original plan. The spectacular *sanktuarium* is seen here before the alterations that followed Vatican II. Although these changes brought a reformed Catholic liturgy, one thing remained—parishioners continue to celebrate Mass at SS. Cyril and Methodius in Polish.

St. Patrick, Lemont's second Irish Catholic church, and the first in town, began as a mission station in "Corkstown," the tent camp for Irish canal workers dating to 1839. The parish built a church on McCarthy Road (then Derby) near Stephen Street in 1862. In 1895, work began on the current limestone edifice, which was based on a plan popular in Ireland.

When this altar was installed in 1917, it was a source of controversy. St. Patrick is known for its beautiful stained-glass windows, with the famous Sullivan family window illuminating the altar. A pastor replaced the window, then erected this elaborate altar modeled after St. Stephen in Vienna, covering the opening. The family protested to the archbishop, who sided with the congregants. The Sullivan window was replaced in 1924.

St. James Academy preceded its neighboring limestone church. The school was begun in 1883 by Rev. J.E. Hogan of St. Patrick Catholic Church. It was the first secondary school in Lemont. Rough-hewn Lemont stone punctuated by tall, regular fenestration gives the block an Italianate flair. The entrance was once topped with a wooden belfry and spire. The building was saved from demolition and is now apartments.

The village's churches are a daily part of life, which is why Lemont is known by many as "The Village of Faith." Situated on Illinois Street just above and to the south of Lemont's commercial core, St. James Academy and St. Patrick Catholic Church keep watch over Main Street. Both still have their original steeples and spires in this view.

Four

WILD MIDWEST

During the early decades of Lemont's development, the Illinois and Michigan Canal was a major transportation route for goods, and Lemont's quarries were the source of its wealth and employment. In July 1839, the paper town of Keepotaw was platted south of the Des Plaines River, which at that time followed its natural course. A month later, the town of Athens was platted and remains as the principal layout of Lemont's oldest sections that grew south from the canal. Lemont's most recognizable and landmark buildings are in its downtown.

The impact of Lemont's limestone industry is found in the commercial and religious buildings made of local stone. The commercial buildings of "Limestone Row" date from 1865 to 1871. Historian Sonia Kallick wrote that in 1870, over 80 percent of the population were unskilled workers, mostly quarrymen, and of these, 80 percent were foreign born. Lemont remained a wild west, a port city reminiscent of a frontier town, with false-front storefronts mixing with cottages and unpaved, muddy streets. Kallick listed "bartender, blacksmith, butcher, carpenter, grocer, and cobbler" among Lemont's business owners, along with other merchants and professionals. By 1880, Lemont's population numbered 2,108 hearty souls, as the town grew south up the valley bluff. Homes from the Victorian era, many in the Queen Anne style, are found on its most important residential street, Singer Avenue.

It was the construction of the Sanitary District of Chicago's drainage canal in the 1890s that had the greatest impact on Lemont's reputation. The town's population surged to nearly 10,000, almost half canal workers. Lemont businesses were ready to offer these workingmen ways to spend. Smokey Row, as Lemont's red-light district was called, was established in the 1860s as a block of frame dives north of the I&M Canal. In the 1890s, vice spread across downtown, centered on Canal Street, to accommodate canal workers. While the nation was suffering an economic bust, Lemont boomed on the revenue of Smokey Row.

On the left in this panoramic view from the 1900s is Lemont's infamous Smokey Row, the early sin strip known for "gambling, liquor, drugs, and women," according to historian Sonia Kallick. The area north of the Santa Fe Railroad tracks in the foreground was known as "the Flats," and hosted horse racing, ball games, carnivals, and gambling. Downtown appears a jumbled mix; typical businesses included hotels, meat markets, and general stores, as well as services such as a tailor,

blacksmith, and druggist. Notable differences from the present include the Santa Fe depot at center, and the corner commanded by the Peiffer-Fischbach Building. On the far right, Lemont Public School (Old Central) looks over town, with the old St. Patrick and Swedish Mission churches nearby.

With the arrival of the Santa Fe Railroad, industry settled north of the Illinois and Michigan Canal. Local breweries were abundant in small towns across America. The Keeley Brewing Company and E. Porter Lemont Branch were both based out of Joliet, as was the Fred Sehring depot seen here, but their products were shipped by rail to Lemont and across the region. With early 20th century technological improvements, Lemont became a popular satellite location for bottling and distribution. The absence of today's Lemont Road High Rise Bridge provides a view of some Singer Avenue

rooftops. Western Stone Company Quarry No. 3, originally established by Nathaniel Brown, can be seen to the right in this panorama. Spires on the left mark the original St. Matthew, SS. Cyril and Methodius, and St. Alphonsus churches.

Limestone buildings are some of the finest—and the village's most memorable—commercial buildings. The north (left) end of this Stephen Street photograph features the demolished Norton's grain elevator, above the canal and next to S.W. Norton's general store. The Fruhauf Building, with the painted ballroom advertisement, began as a saloon. The corner Anderson Building/Odin Hall also started as a saloon, but here, it is the post office.

Fine wines, liquors, and beer were necessities available for sale in this early photograph of the Fruhauf Building at the northeast corner of Stephen and Talcott Streets. Lemont in the 19th century was "ground zero . . . where half the aldermen were saloon keepers and about a hundred dance halls, gambling dens, saloons, and bawdy houses ran day and night," according to *The Lost Panoramas*.

Lemonters take a unique pride in Smokey Row. Not much in the way of furnishings was needed to satisfy the drinking demands of patrons, and given the era's reputation for violence, less was likely better. There were no stools, and patrons used a foot rail at this saloon, operated by John Powalisz. While an electric light was present, a potbelly stove and heavy jackets were still required.

In its heyday, Lemonters could stand anywhere downtown and be no more than 500 feet away from a tavern. These men (and a boy!) hold their drinks in a toast for the photograph. This bar was in the basement of the Peiffer and Fischbach Building at Canal and Lemont Streets, below Bodenschatz drugstore.

In this rare view looking south on Lemont Street, most buildings still stand today, including what is now Main Inn (center), St. Matthew Evangelical Lutheran Church (with original spire), the Old Stone Church, and Bethany Lutheran. The Peiffer and Fischbach Building—seen prominently here at the corner of Lemont and Canal Streets—was demolished in 1974. The brick building at Lemont and Illinois Streets was known as Otzenberger Hall.

This photograph of the corner bay of the Peiffer and Fischbach Building shows the unique brick masonry, stonework, and metal cornice that decorated the turret on the northwest corner of the building. It was the tallest building north of Main Street and was a fixture throughout its existence, with its cupola visible in many early views of Lemont's business district.

Canal Street between Stephen and Lemont Streets looks relatively similar today, although there are several differences. Tedens Insurance was on the southwest corner (mostly cropped in this photograph), and Fischbach's turret is visible at the western end of the block. J.G. Bodenschatz was the Deutsche Apotheke (pharmacy), evidence of Lemont's prominent German community. Tedens would later operate a drugstore at this corner.

What seems like a peculiar arrangement on the west side of Stephen Street, with four frame buildings at an angle to the right of way, is actually a remnant of Lemont's first town plat, Keepotaw. These early buildings stand in contrast to Limestone Row across the street. Several buildings on the north side of Canal Street follow the same original town plat.

The original Tedens and Company dry goods store is seen here in 1875. This building stood at 106 Stephen Street before it was doubled in size. The expansion was necessary due to the amount of goods available from the Illinois and Michigan Canal. Tedens's location made it possible to receive products directly from the canal in its early days.

In 1895, the Tedens building was extended to 10 bays wide, with fenestration that mirrored the original building. Queen Anne–style ornamentation, with a decorative metal pediment, cornice, and cartouche, topped where the old and new met. On the second floor, Tedens Opera House presented live entertainment and movies. Posters for silent movies date this image to 1921.

Plenty of merchandise was on display at Tedens and Dystrop in 1912, but patrons were required to pay cash. "Positively No Trust" comes from Herman Melville's 1857 novel *The Confidence Man*, in which a scammer on a steamboat separates people from their money. This slogan meant that goods and services required immediate payment, with no open tabs for customers.

Entertainment options were not limited to Smokey Row's sin and taverns. Dance halls, bowling alleys, and venues for musical performers, comedies, and theater could be found on every street, often on the second floor of a larger building. In the Smokey Row era, dancing girls could be found at Kimek's, where it cost a dime to view the show. This photograph dates to about 1930.

This photograph from about 1899 features an intersection of Main and State Streets that no longer exists. A stone sidewalk is visible in front of Marble City House. Limestone flagging was a popular product from Lemont quarries in the limestone era. Home and store builders frequently used local materials in their construction. The electric company came to Lemont in 1893, which also provided street lighting.

A decade later, this eastward view on Main Street shows how quickly the town was changing. When the Lemont Road High Rise Bridge was constructed in the 1980s, several of these buildings, including this handsome corner saloon, were demolished. Built in the 1900s, John Peterson's corner tavern served a popular Swedish smorgasbord. Its last tenant before demolition was Matt's Inn.

The Marble City House, run by the New family, was described as the classiest saloon in town at one time. Living quarters were above the first floor. Advertising shows they served beer from E. Porter Brewing in Joliet. Nicholas New was elected trustee in Lemont's first village election in 1873. At this corner, Main Street becomes New Avenue as it heads west.

Smokey Row provided lucrative business for the young village government, with liquor license fees bringing in enough revenue to build a limestone village hall in 1893. It shared this stretch of Main Street with a tailor, saloon, grocer, and another saloon. It was said the village licensed 40 saloons, and another 40 operated unlicensed. A liquor license cost $500, the equivalent of $18,000 today.

The Budnik Building at the corner of Stephen and Main Streets was adjacent to the former Chicago & Joliet Electric Railway. Budnik had previously operated a few blocks west until construction of the current brick building was completed on January 29, 1927. The Classical Revival building is the most decorated brickwork structure remaining downtown.

Here are Stephen and Main Streets, looking west around 1912. The east-facing false front of Wend's is visible on the left, and the railroad tower that stood between the Chicago & Alton Railroad and Chicago & Joliet Electric Railway was still operational. A man stands against a utility pole, presumably waiting for a streetcar toward Chicago.

When the village of Keepotaw was platted, streets were oriented north and south. Three of these early blocks remain downtown, at a noticeable angle to the current street grid, which was reoriented to the canal with the town of Athens. This 1894 map identifies just 24 of the many saloons in Lemont. (Courtesy of Library of Congress.)

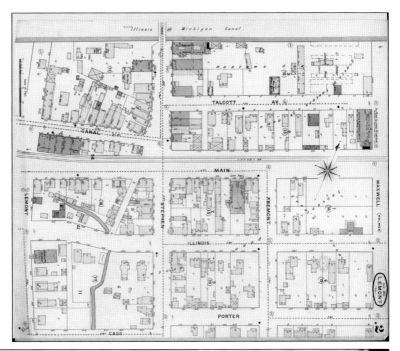

Not all merchants were in Lemont's central business district. Several shops opened along the square across from SS. Cyril and Methodius to supply Lemont's large Polish community. Joseph Krumray's groceries, flour, and feed store was one of them, with the extended family posing in front of their shop. It stood at the corner of Sobieski and Czacki Streets, with their home connected next door.

Singer Avenue, named for quarry magnate Horace M. Singer, runs parallel to State Street from Cass Street through Peiffer Avenue. It is often considered the most architecturally significant street in town and is part of the Lemont Historic District. This view looking north shows Singer Avenue following the valley into town, between Custer and Division Streets. Note the carriage step on the left side of the street.

Singer Avenue features a diverse range of architecturally significant homes. The foursquare at 506 (left) and the Queen Anne at 504 (right), both from the 1890s, are still standing and appear nearly identical a century later. After the boundaries of Lemont's historic district were established, residents petitioned to include the 400 to 800 blocks of Singer Avenue within it.

Most of Lemont's decorated Victorian mansions can be found on Singer Avenue, although several were found throughout other parts of town. This house on the 800 block of State Street is still standing; however, its appearance has been significantly altered. It is presently an American foursquare and was remodeled following a second-story fire.

Neighborhoods in Lemont developed around different hills. Singer Hill, from Division Street to Peiffer Avenue and State Street to Warner Avenue, contained a small commercial district at State Street and Eureka Drive. This photograph shows a delivery wagon waiting near Singer Hill Grocery. There was also a fix-it shop, a bowling alley, a laundry, and Firehouse No. 2 with its hose cart. (Courtesy of Barb Bannon.)

Peter Mirkes is pictured inside Singer Hill Grocery in 1930. Mirkes inherited the business and building at 801 State Street from his father, Theodore, in 1910. Neighborhood stores supplied goods within walking distance of residential areas, saving a trip downtown in an era before automobile ownership became common. A rear addition to the building around 1936 included a billiards room. (Courtesy of Barb Bannon.)

One door north of Singer Hill Grocery in an unnumbered single-story building was Art Steinke's barbershop, built right up to the sidewalk. His business was originally downtown on Main Street before relocating up Singer Hill. Haircuts with tonic were 35¢, and a shave was 15¢, with wax for mustaches as needed. This building still stands on State Street today.

Illinois Street runs 12 blocks east to west, intersecting Stephen and State Streets. Illinois Street east of Stephen Street, as seen here, features many vernacular homes from the 19th century and is included in the Lemont Historic District. Notable residents on Illinois Street included Sylvester Derby, Lemuel Brown, Doctor Ludwig, and John Bodenschatz, among others.

The Bodenschatz house, at 311 East Illinois Street, is seen here with members of the family posing outside. The palms on the porch and bird cage out front are both Victorian in fashion. John G. Bodenschatz purchased his drugstore on Stephen Street from a cousin after 1873. Bodenschatz was a member of the Knights of Pythias and a volunteer firefighter.

Most residents lived in houses similar to this 19th-century vernacular-style home on Porter Street. Since roads were not yet paved at the time, wooden sidewalks were prevalent. A quick walk through Singer's Hill, Jasnagora, and throughout Lemont's old town will find similar modest homes.

Here is a scene at Hermes farm, once located in Sag near the border of Lemont and Palos Townships. This early 20th century photograph is a reminder that much of the area surrounding Lemont was once rural. This farm would later become Kopping Farms Equestrian Center and the residential community of Equestrian Estates.

John Hescher pauses in his labor to show sheep and goats on his farm at Warner and Peiffer Avenues in the 1920s. Livestock grazed in all areas surrounding the village. This farm was at the previous village limits, now a residential and commercial area.

Farm scenes like this were common surrounding the village of Lemont, with vintage and antique tractors still a popular draw at local events. Farming families in Lemont Township had diverse livestock, and many raised dairy cows, cattle, hogs, and chickens, plus vegetables, hay, and corn. Railroads helped bring their products to Chicago's markets.

Nathaniel J. Brown is seen on the bluff overlooking his farm about a mile west of town. Athens marble from his quarries was used to build barns on the property and was donated to the Methodist Episcopal church, where he was a prominent member. Brown was born in Vermont and moved to New York as a child, and later to Michigan while it was still a US territory. As a young man, he bought property there and opened a sawmill on 900 acres. Brown shipped the first load of lumber from Grand Haven to Chicago, arriving in April 1835. He stayed in the city, and with the money he earned from his cargo, began purchasing real estate. In 1837, Brown was awarded a contract to excavate a mile of the Illinois and Michigan Canal at present-day Lemont. When finished, he made Lemont his home. Most of the real estate Brown owned in Lemont was quarries he helped discover while building the canal. Brown owned three quarries, leasing two to builders.

Five

A VILLAGE TAKES ROOT

Lemont is a community devoted to preservation while progressing forward with new development. In its earliest days, log cabins were not only homes but also places of worship. Canal workers lived in temporary locations, but as laborers became permanent residents, the need for various community institutions and businesses that served residents became apparent—not just the needs of Smokey Row. While saloons remained plentiful downtown, Lemont residents became engaged in trades that served the "honest" residents. Church parishes established commanding limestone houses of worship, schools were built, and signs of a lasting population began to shape the community.

Lemont became an incorporated village on June 9, 1873, by a vote of 243-0. The first village elections were held that August. During the following decades, the village would transform from a quarry town to a canal town and back, see Smokey Row grow and go bust, and build some of its finest institutional structures. The village hall, waterworks, and Lemont Public School were all constructed of local limestone in the last half of the 19th century and remain landmarks in town.

Civic life and social organizations flourished in this golden era of fraternalism. The community frequently came together for parades and processions. Organizations such as the volunteer fire department were established, with Germans leading hose Company No. 1, and Irishmen manning hook-and-ladder Company No. 2.

By the 1920s, Lemont saw the arrival of major religious retreats on old farmlands east of the village limits. Mount Assisi Convent and Academy, St. Mary's Monastery and Retreat House, Our Lady of Victory Convent and Franciscan Village, and the Fournier Institute and St. Vincent DePaul Seminary, now the Lithuanian World Center, all date from this period. These institutions have had a lasting impact on village life that continues today. Forest preserves, golf courses, cemeteries, and other large landholders began to ring the tiny village.

Lemont Village Hall was built in 1893, designed by architect Hugo Boehme of Joliet in the Richardsonian Romanesque style, which highlights the beauty of Lemont limestone. This building has housed police and fire departments, as well as Lemont's library and American Legion. The wood bell tower has since been lost, but the building continues to serve as the seat of village government at 418 Main Street.

John McCarthy, village president, stands at far left in front of village hall in the 1890s with members of Lemont's volunteer fire department. The men with the "2HL" logos on their uniforms are members of the second hook-and-ladder company. A truck and hose cart were stationed behind the double doors at village hall. There were no paved roads, and equipment was pulled by hand.

The late 19th century was an era of extensive village improvements. Water mains were built between 1883 and 1885. The Village of Lemont Waterworks Building, constructed at 43 Stephen Street in 1891, was north of the canal. Sparse in ornamentation, the building highlights the bold use of rusticated Lemont limestone, and later housed the Lemont Power and Light Company. (Courtesy of the Metropolitan Water Reclamation District of Greater Chicago.)

Lemont residents pack St. Patrick Catholic Church for the funeral of Mayor John McCarthy. There are two streets in Lemont named for McCarthy, a testament to his influence and popularity. He moved to Lemont in 1858, married a local girl, and was an attorney, real estate developer, and civic leader. McCarthy was school board clerk, township supervisor during the time of the quarry strikes, and served four terms as mayor.

Stephen Street had a mix of shops that served the community. Lemont Bakery began next door in the one-story building that has since been demolished, and moved into the well-detailed brick structure at right sometime after 1894. It still stands at 202 Stephen Street, although with an Art Deco–inspired re-face. Down the street, butchers stand outside Frank Sniegowski's shop, which later became Midwest Grocery.

Businesses in these days were heavily focused on local owners, producers, and manufacturers. In this photograph, Ernest William Kollman carries fresh loaves of bread for delivery from his wagon sometime in the 1920s. The Kollman Brothers Bakery was on Stephen Street, which at various times had four bakeries on this single block.

Burr Oak Farm Dairy was one of many that delivered dairy products directly to Lemont residents. The "pure milk," seen here carried by owner George Ahrens, is in pasteurized bottles. "Fresh from the farm" did not mean raw milk, as pasteurization was a health crusade of the era, with Lemont schoolchildren joining the movement. This photograph was taken in the 1920s.

Workers pose with milk cans and bottles at the Lemont Dairy, west of one of the depots. Owned by the Skrzypkowski family, the stacks of milk cans and their depot location suggest they were shipping milk to Chicago dairies, while the men holding pasteurized bottles hint they may be processing the milk in Lemont.

Lemont's first public school was built in 1869 with local limestone. It housed four graded classrooms until the 1890s, when Lemont's population doubled, requiring the school board to let out bids for an addition. The clock tower, which must have been a prominent feature from all corners of Lemont, was removed with the addition.

Students are dressed uniformly for graduation day in front of the public "graded school," as the original Central School was called. The photograph reveals the contrast in style between the two buildings, with smooth stone enhanced by rough block quoining on the corners, and the use of a mixed bond of irregular shaped stones, similar to the Methodist Episcopal church.

Public School, Lemont, Ill.

In 1896, the school was expanded. This remarkable addition to Lemont Public School was designed by architect John Barnes of Joliet. It was completed in the Richardsonian style, with rough-hewn Lemont limestone contrasting with the smooth cuts of the earlier school. It included space for a high school and served as such until 1922. All eight grades were offered in these buildings until the 1950s.

In this class photograph from the 1890s, students and their teachers pose in front of the impressive entrance to the new public school. The deeply recessed entryway highlights the finest qualities of the local limestone and the craftsmanship of Lemont's quarry workers. Limestone was dressed, turned, and carved, transforming the stone into blocks, pillars, and cornices.

758

The majestic architecture of "Old Central" School contrasts with the dirt road and utilitarian street lighting of early Lemont. To the east (left) of the school is the first St. Patrick church, built in 1862. Across the road, known then as Prairie Avenue, and before that Derby, is the Swedish Mission church.

Originally located at the corner of McCarthy Road and Fremont Street was the Swedish Mission church. The parish's attendance regressed when many Swedish Lemonters joined Bethany Lutheran Church instead. The lumber from this church was repurposed to construct a two-flat home on Holmes Street, while ash trees planted by Swedish immigrants remained on this site for decades to follow.

Lemont high school students are pictured in 1919 in the old public school. Lemont Township High School began in 1906 with just five students. The high school district leased three rooms on the second floor of the old limestone school on McCarthy Road. The National Register of Historic Places claims this was one of the oldest continuously used schools in the state of Illinois.

Lemont Township High School's first basketball team is pictured in 1916. This photograph can be seen hanging in the classroom image above, at right. Lemont played independent teams this first season, and its only high school opponent was Lockport. Without a sports conference, Lemont basketball was often described as David taking on Goliath. Joliet Catholic, Hinsdale, and Joliet Township were all early foes.

John Doolin presides over a combined fifth-and-sixth grade at Lemont Public School in 1922. Doolin was also a school board member and township assessor. He worked and wrote passionately to convince voters to approve a high school referendum. Lessons from over a century ago can just barely be made out on the blackboards. There are 35 students in this class photograph.

As the graded classes grew, the high school was forced out of the old public school. The following year, each grade had its own classroom. By 1923, Lemont high school students had their classes in "portables," after losing their space in Old Central in 1922, hence the makeshift architecture and large cast-iron heater seen here. Students would remain here until May 1925.

Despite its beauty, Old Central School was closed due to the need for a larger and safer building. The fire escape slide from the second floor seen here was added for emergency purposes. Older residents remember the thrill of rushing down this slide. The building was saved from demolition by the Save Our School committee in the 1970s and redeveloped as residences in the 1980s.

This 1956 picture, taken in a classroom of the old Lemont Public School, shows students smiling. Students had good reason to be happy. That year, an addition added new classrooms, a gymnasium, lockers, and an administrative office. Classrooms in the historic building were renovated while the new Central School was constructed next door, connecting to the old building. For some time, classes were held in both buildings.

Lemont Township High School opened in 1925. On September 22, 1923, voters approved a referendum for a new high school at 800 Porter Street, where the high school still stands. Construction started in 1924 on the original 18,000 square feet school building, which began with eight classrooms, a library, science and home economics labs, and a gymnasium.

Graduating seniors, 28 in all, from Lemont Township High School pose for a class photograph in 1929. This class was the first to attend all four years at LTHS, starting as freshmen in 1926. The school had opened before the close of the school year in 1925, making that class the first to graduate.

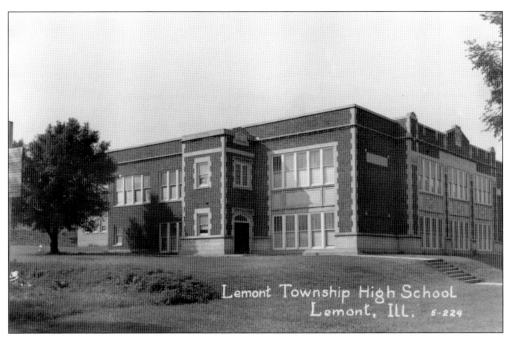

In 1927, additional lots around the high school were purchased, extending the campus to 6.5 acres. A corner of the old scoreboard is at far left, indicating the need for the extra space. The original school stood on just five lots. The expanded campus allowed the school to build its home ball fields.

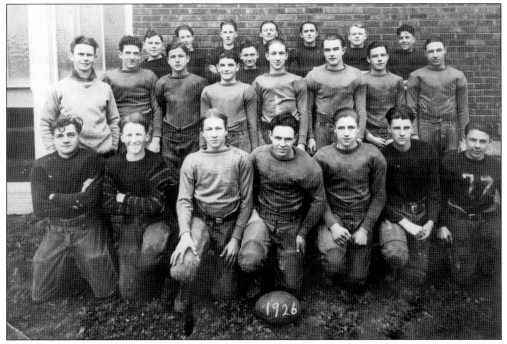

The Lemont Township High School football team poses proudly in front of its new home in 1926, the first season played at Porter Street. The football program began in 1921 while still in portable classrooms on McCarthy Road. The golden years for Lemont football were said to be 1950–1952, when the team had a 21-1-1 overall record.

Mount Assisi Academy was started by the School Sisters of St. Francis of Christ the King as a college preparatory, all-girl Catholic high school. The academy building opened in September 1955, with 80 students that inaugural year. Mount Assisi Academy closed permanently in 2014, although events and activities are still hosted here today.

The School Sisters of St. Francis of Christ the King came to Lemont in 1925, purchasing a 26-acre farm atop the hills overlooking the Des Plaines River valley. With an increase in sisters, the building pictured here was dedicated in 1941. Mount Assisi Academy was established in 1951 with six classrooms in this convent.

The Slovenian Franciscan Friars of the Custody of the Holy Cross came to Lemont in 1924, naming their monastery St. Mary's. A seminary was dedicated in 1940, serving that role until 1956. As a mission center for Slovenians, the guest house, built in 1946, continues to schedule retreats, and the monastery operates as a mission parish. The grounds are landscaped with a grotto, shrine, pond, and other religious stations.

The cornerstone for Our Lady of Victory Convent was set in 1936. The Franciscan Sisters of Chicago lived in this building until 1963, when a new motherhouse opened and this became Mother Theresa Home. They had purchased the Walker estate in 1925 and his old mansion was used as a novitiate. Venerable Mother Mary Theresa Dudzik is interred here at the Sacred Heart Chapel.

The Keepotaw Lodge of the Knights of Pythias was a secret society that began in 1890. Their Castle Hall was on the second floor of the Fruhauf Building. While their happenings remain a secret, their charter members were a "who's who" of turn-of-the-century Lemont, with names like Norton, Nelson, Wold, Earnshaw, Reis, Meyer, Warner, Bodenschatz, Kettering, Losey, Friedley, and several village trustees.

Not all societies were quite so strict, although their purpose may still remain a mystery today. The Lemont Outing Club poses with a bold L.O.C. Club pennant, with most members holding a beverage in their hands and a case of bottles between them. Lemont residents could find almost any kind of club that interested them.

The Lemont Citizens Band poses after taking first prize in a competition. Musicians were always ready to perform for the many Lemont celebrations, parades, and dedications. The Lemont Citizens Band appears to be the earliest, later known as the Lemont Municipal Band. There was also a Lemont Brass Band and a Lemont Children's Band, among many others.

Lemont Township High School sophomores pose in front of village hall in a formation that spells L E M O N T. This photograph was taken as Lemont celebrated a big fall festival, with three days of floats, bands, entertainment, and prizes. This demonstrated the love and community Lemont residents felt that made their little town special.

The color guard from the American Legion Lemont Post No. 243 marches on Lockport Street ahead of a funeral procession through village park. In 1919, Lemont veterans held a meeting at village hall to form a legion post. The American Legion continued to host events in Lemont for decades, with the post providing a firing squad and a drum and bugle corps. This procession captures a lost scene on Lockport Street, with a view of the park in the background and Bromberg's Dairy to the right of the marchers. In 1937, the American Legion dedicated a field piece in the village park. In turn, the village gifted the park to the Legion, and it has been known as American Legion Park since, now part of the Lemont Park District.

Six

TRANSPORTATION AND TRANSFORMATION

The history and architecture of Lemont are tied to its canals, railroads, roads, and highways. Several waterways replaced the shallow Des Plaines River through Lemont's history, starting with the Illinois and Michigan Canal, the Chicago Sanitary and Ship Canal, and eventually the Cal-Sag Channel. The Alton, Chicago & St. Louis Railroad began construction in 1847, reaching Chicago by 1858, and provided passenger rail service and the transportation of agricultural products. The Chicago & Alton depot is still in use by Metra, and proudly proclaims it as the oldest of its over 240 active stations throughout Chicagoland. The Atchison, Topeka & Santa Fe Railway arrived in 1886 and provided freight service and a depot. By 1930, the I&M Canal was often dry and no longer saw commercial use from Joliet to Chicago following the opening of the Sanitary District of Chicago's drainage canal in 1900.

As the town's reliance on the I&M Canal lessened, it saw a more diversified use of its land. Development of downtown began to spread outward along its western half, where the depots were located. Large-scale manufacturing such as Illinois Pure Aluminum Company, soda and beer bottling companies, and clothing and shoe manufacturing businesses lined the railroads and helped keep jobs in Lemont as the quarries declined. The shift in transportation to personal vehicles brought major energy firms to Lemont's borders, with oil companies lined up along the Chicago Sanitary and Ship Canal, which remains an active industrial port.

The evolution from horse-drawn transportation to the automobile changed the town's development patterns. New commuter service was available on light rail through the Chicago & Joliet Electric Railway by the beginning of the 20th century, built directly over Main Street and terminating in Chicago via the city's oldest road, Archer Avenue. The streets in Lemont were finally paved. Gas stations, garages, and showrooms opened in downtown Lemont. State highways reached town, and Main and State Streets became major thoroughfares. Lemont's growth—residential, industrial, and institutional—expanded.

The Chicago, Alton & St. Louis Railroad, the first to arrive in Lemont, was completed in 1858. In addition to daily passenger service, the railroad spurred the growth of Lemont farm business. A livestock yard was kept by the railroad for steers and pigs to be sent to the stockyards, and the "milk train" would bring 300-500 cans to Chicago dairies.

The Chicago & Alton Lemont station has been recognized as the oldest masonry depot in Chicagoland. Built of Athens marble, this historical and architecturally significant station opened in 1858 and has been serving commuters ever since. It is now managed by Metra, and is the oldest station in its system. Pres. Abraham Lincoln's funeral train passed through Lemont along these tracks on the evening of May 2, 1865.

A Wells Fargo wagon waits at the Atchison, Topeka & Santa Fe depot, built in 1886. Primarily serving freight traffic, the Santa Fe offered occasional passenger service as well. Its depot was north of the Illinois and Michigan Canal, where River Street is today. Its tracks had to be realigned with the construction of the drainage canal. This depot was demolished for the Lemont Road High Rise Bridge.

The Santa Fe Bridge is a two-track, bobtail swing bridge; its turntable is visible under the bridge on the north bank of the canal. To the west, the Stephen Street Bridge carried vehicle traffic and was of a similar design. The Stephen Street Bridge was replaced with the Lemont Road High Rise Bridge, but the Santa Fe Bridge remains busy with rail traffic today.

Stephen Street was once a main artery through Lemont, but not since the Lemont Road High Rise Bridge opened in 1984. This photograph shows the original wood plank deck that horses, and later automobiles, used. In the distance, Lemont Road curves as it climbs the north bluff of the Des Plaines River valley. (Courtesy of the Metropolitan Water Reclamation District of Greater Chicago.)

This postcard shows a view looking east from the north bank of the Chicago Drainage Canal with the Stephen Street Bridge in the foreground and Santa Fe behind. The Sanitary District of Chicago built multiple bridges of this type during this era. One can still traverse this type of bridge on the Centennial Trail at Schneider's Passage, where the identical Romeo Road Bridge was repurposed for recreation.

In 1901, the Chicago & Joliet Electric Railway ran north from Joliet into Lemont. The following year, it reached Chicago through Summit and offered connection service to the Chicago Surface Line at Archer and Cicero Avenues. Built before Lemont had paved roads, the tracks entered town on Main Street and merged onto New Avenue before continuing southwest.

This impressive and imposing station, a mix of European influences and styles, hides an incredible substation used to help power the electric railway. The smaller garage to the west of the building is all that remains, its outline perceptible facing New Avenue. The Chicago & Joliet Electric Railway operated in Lemont until 1933.

The 20th century saw the opening of a third canal, the Cal-Sag Channel. Its confluence with the Chicago Sanitary and Ship Canal, seen here, is the western point of Mount Forest Island. These manmade waterways followed ancient river routes that shaped the landscape of Lemont and Chicagoland. Tugboats operated on oil fuel with diesel engines, a powerful upgrade over steam. (Courtesy of the Metropolitan Water Reclamation District of Greater Chicago.)

Lemont's three historic canals converge in this photograph of the Calumet-Sag crossing the Illinois and Michigan Canal, which ran parallel to the Chicago Drainage Canal in the background. Water from the Sanitary District of Chicago's channels flows into the I&M Canal. This photograph is roughly where Sidestream Elevated Pool Aeration Station No. 5 is today. (Courtesy of the Metropolitan Water Reclamation District of Greater Chicago.)

After the opening of the Chicago Sanitary and Ship Canal, commercial industries in downtown Lemont clung on along the Illinois and Michigan Canal. Along the canal near State Street, industry repurposed what were once quarry sites, such as this construction supply scene. As water levels on the canal began to drop, Lemont's two railroads became the lifeblood of local industry.

With the opening of the Chicago Sanitary and Ship Canal in 1900, the Illinois and Michigan Canal, once the heart of Lemont, slowly trickled through the canal towns from Joliet to Chicago. Feeder canals that were needed to keep the Illinois and Michigan Canal navigable failed, and by the 20th century, it was unusable north of Joliet. (Courtesy of the Metropolitan Water Reclamation District of Greater Chicago.)

Lemont's military history dates to the US Civil War, and residents have volunteered in every US conflict since 1861. The men gathered here were preparing for the trip to Europe at the start of World War I. Onlookers lean out of village hall's windows as some of these Lemonters took a final photograph before leaving to fight.

Parades during the war years were enthusiastic, brimming with patriotic support for the nation and Lemont's "boys" in World War I. Men, women, and children all participated in this parade on Main Street, seen here near Lemont Street. Lemont residents joined in the ecstatic celebration sweeping the world when the Great War truce was announced on November 11, 1918, Armistice Day.

Members of the American Legion salute Lemont's unknown soldier on Memorial Day in the Danish Cemetery. On July 1, 1919, a uniformed soldier was found dead in the canal. He was buried here by American Legion Post No. 243 with military honors. Later, the site became a memorial to all unknown soldiers, with a gravestone designed to resemble the Washington Monument. Anderson Lodge No. 52 bought this land for burials in 1892.

The Veterans of Foreign Wars was organized shortly after World War II. Local members held an opening meeting in February 1946 and selected the name Lemont 22 Honor Post No. 5819. The earliest meetings were held at village hall until this clubroom at 112 Stephen Street opened in July 1948. The post moved to its present location on New Avenue in August 1951.

The Civilian Conservation Corps (CCC) was established to provide employment to young men during the Great Depression. Camp Lemont-Brandon, seen here near Romeo, built the Illinois and Michigan Canal Parkway, the statewide trail still in use today. Other Lemont camps were located in "Sag Forest" and built county parks. Waterfall Glen, Black Partridge Woods, and Swallow Cliff toboggan slides are part of their lasting legacy.

Men in the CCC lived in military-style camps with large barracks built by each company. They were paid $30 a month, with $25 sent back to their family. From 1933 to 1942, the CCC provided work and training in environmental conservation and natural resource management, and constructed many parks, trails, and other public works projects.

The US Postal Service's first permanent location in downtown at 42 Stephen Street is still in use. Architect Louis A. Simon designed the building in the Art Deco style. The post office was dedicated on Independence Day 1937. Inside is a 1938 Works Progress Administration (WPA) mural, *Canal Boats*, by Charles Turzak.

In the 1920s, the village board approved new sewer and water mains. The department of streets and alleys supervised the paving. Here, a steamroller stands by on Stephen Street as a Santa Fe train passes overhead. Early automobiles can be seen in the shadows on the road leading to the Stephen Street Bridge, with decorative walls built from rough limestone blocks.

Recreation Bowl
Lemont, Ill. s-225

Many Lemonters recall sports and social activities in "the Bowl," the recreation area south of Old Central School. A project of the Civil Works Authority, its construction in the 1930s put nearly 300 locals to work during the Depression. A ball field was cleared, the site was graded for bleachers and a toboggan slide, and a bandstand called the Castle was built. The Lemont Recreation Bowl was dedicated in 1938.

The Bowl was in a natural glacial sag formed from melting ice. During its 1933 construction, Native American skeletons, a calumet, and numerous artifacts were discovered, leading early excavators to believe this was once a Potawatomi encampment site. The WPA project improved the drainage that directed stormwater into the Illinois and Michigan Canal, and continues to do so today.

At one time, business-backed sports teams thrived in Lemont. Blesch and Welter led the way, sponsoring a bowling league, basketball team, and a semiprofessional baseball team, seen here at the Bowl in 1940. The Lumbermen was a clever name, since Blesch and Welter operated a lumber and building materials yard at 106 Stephen Street. One of their uniforms is displayed at the Lemont Area Historical Society museum.

Another men's team poses for a photograph, the location identified by the Fred Sehring beer depot and Santa Fe Railroad in the background. Baseball was not limited to the Bowl, and fields could be found throughout town. This was "the Flats," where there was a game every Sunday and teams played for a purse of $40 to $60. For the fans, beer cost a nickel.

John Roebuck's service station was previously located at 225 East Illinois Street. As motoring moved from a hobby to a popular mode of transportation, auto-oriented businesses followed in Lemont. The shift to the automobile expanded the existing downtown, as Lemont opened three gas stations, two dealerships, and several garages and service stations.

Here is a glimpse of Toddle Grove, a dance hall on State Street south of Lemont's village limits, which opened in 1921. The *Lemont Optimist-News* gushed, "Lemont is indeed fortunate in having this amusement center at her door, and should be patronized by all who trip the light fantastic." Amusement pavilions were popular destinations for dancing and socializing at that time.

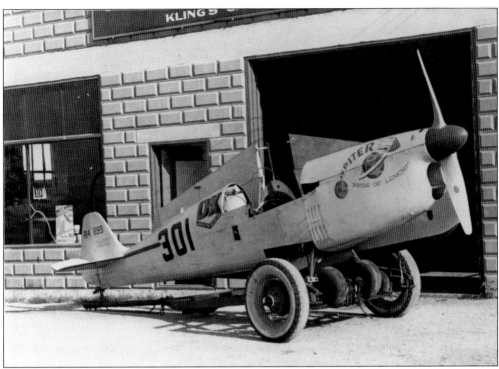

Rudy Kling was born in 1908 to German immigrants in DuPage County. Twenty years later, his first garage opened on a wagon route turned multistate highway, Route 66. Kling's aviation skills were apparent from his first race, which he not only easily won, but set the then-record for light planes, flying at 228.07 miles per hour. Kling named his SK-3 plane *Jupiter, the Pride of Lemont*.

Rudy and Theresa Kling pose at the 1937 National Air Races, held on Labor Day in Cleveland, Ohio. That day, Kling won, from left to right, the Greve Trophy, Thompson Trophy, and the Henderson Merit Award, after earning first place while reaching 256.9 miles per hour. Rudy Kling died in an air race crash in Miami later that year, on December 3, 1937, his 29th birthday.

Illinois Pure Aluminum Company, at the southwest corner of Holmes and Talcott Streets, was established in 1892 and was the oldest manufacturer of spun aluminum cookware in the United States. Products were marketed under the name Walker Ware, named for owner George Walker. He bought the company with money raised from his many local quarries after the original owners defaulted.

"The ware that wears" was an iconic industry in Lemont. This view looking north on Holmes Street south of the Chicago & Alton Railroad shows where the cookware was produced. The building on the east (right) side of the compound was a lumberyard, and the administration office pictured above can be seen facing west in the background.

Illinois Pure Aluminum received national attention during the 1893 World's Columbian Exposition in Chicago and changed how Americans prepared meals in their homes. It was the high-tech industry of its era and remained a successful business in Lemont for many decades until its end in 1977. This photograph, taken in 1985, shows the last iteration of the warehouse before its demolition.

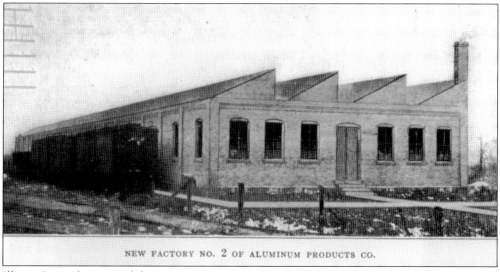

NEW FACTORY NO. 2 OF ALUMINUM PRODUCTS CO.

Illinois Pure Aluminum did not maintain a monopoly on aluminum production, as the Aluminum Products Company, based out of LaGrange, expanded with a second factory on New Avenue in the 1910s. It was eventually purchased by Reynolds Metals Company, which continued to operate Plant No. 2. A careful eye can still identify this plant on New Avenue west of downtown Lemont.

Lemont Pants was a local, family-owned manufacturing company, begun by Peter Kluge when he was just 20 years old. The company specialized in wholesale orders. Lemont's centennial book stated that more than 1,500,000 pairs of pants left the factory at 310 East Illinois Street, which still stands today.

The Fournier Institute, later to become St. Vincent De Paul Seminary, was initially a retirement home for priests. It was purchased by entrepreneur and philanthropist Arthur Schmidt in the 1940s who established the Fournier Institute of Technology, providing pre-engineering and training in various fields until its closure in 1955. This campus was eventually demolished in 1996; the remainder of Schmidt's estate housed the DeAndreis Seminary.

DeAndreis Seminary opened in 1964 near 127th Street. Its modernist, steeply pitched roof can be seen throughout Lemont. After its sale in the mid-1980s to Lithuanian investors, it has been known as the Lithuanian World Center. Lemont already had a sizable Lithuanian community. A school began as early as 1959, teaching language and folkloric customs, and graduates continue to bring their children to Lemont every Saturday.

The Pure Oil Company traces its roots to 1922, giving jobs to generations of Lemonters, first as Lemont Refining Company, then Globe Oil and Refining, Union Oil, Uno-Ven, and now CITGO Lemont Refinery. The early Globe Oil was once the largest refinery in Illinois. When Pure Oil purchased the company in 1954, it was producing 47,500 barrels a day.

The first Argonne Laboratory was located in Cook County's Argonne Forest preserve, three miles southeast of the present site, now Red Gate Woods. After the first controlled nuclear chain reaction at the University of Chicago, the research was moved here in 1943. As part of the Manhattan Project, the site provided necessary seclusion. This laboratory designed and built Chicago Pile No. 3, the world's first heavy-water moderated reactor.

Argonne National Laboratory was chartered in 1946 and chose Lemont to build the first national laboratory in America. Today, Argonne scientists conduct research in a wide range of fields, including nuclear energy, physics, chemistry, materials science, and computer science. This aerial view highlights Argonne's secluded setting. The facility occupies 3,700 acres. Argonne's famous "white deer" were left behind by a former estate owner.

Seven

KEEP THE FAITH

"Lemont, the Village of Faith" has been a popular motto for longtime Lemonters, one that refuses to disappear. Many count their time in Lemont by generations. They keep the memories of days gone by alive by faith in their community.

Lemont's development into a suburb of Chicago became inevitable during the 20th century. By the 1980s, the isolated town in the hills, protected by forests and waterways, had been discovered. Because Lemont's identity had been so strongly written through the hardworking men and women who created this town by digging a canal through bedrock, it has a presence that can never be lost. A walk through Lemont is a reminder of their faith; at times, the aura of their ghosts can be felt.

In addition to the original Seven Steeples, other congregations have served Lemont, along with several parochial schools. Lemont Township, the first form of governance, continues to serve Lemont's residents. As the town grew, the township saw the need for parks and helped establish the Lemont Park District. A library that began in village hall is now the Lemont Public Library District. Lemont's fire department evolved from a group of volunteers to a full-time department and later the Lemont Fire Protection District. Each of these organizations has its own unique history.

Over several decades and the efforts of many, there has been an ongoing interest in Lemont's revitalization potential. Efforts have been made to preserve and restore historic buildings throughout downtown, and new businesses have moved in to take advantage of the area's unique character and location. Today, Lemont is a charming and vibrant mix of historic buildings and new businesses that cater to the needs of residents and visitors alike. Lemont offers something for everyone and is a testament to the town's long history and ongoing evolution.

Here is downtown Lemont, looking southeast from the high bridge over Main Street, featuring church steeples and spires on the peaks of hills, complemented by the imposing Old Central School. For many, this view is their first impression of town. For others who call Lemont home, it is a proud reminder of the village's unique charm and a connection to its past.

This is Lemont viewed from the Stephen Street Bridge about 1964. Prior to the Lemont Road High Rise Bridge, this two-lane road was the only way across the waterways and into town. While the metal truss Stephen Street Bridge was demolished in the 1980s, Old Lemont Road was rebuilt and still crosses the Des Plaines River, now used for industrial traffic.

"View from Budnik Plaza" is an original watercolor by Lemont artist Joyce Affelt. She began with art lessons at the Lemont Park District. Locals loved her painted scenes of downtown Lemont businesses and many churches. Affelt's work artfully captures a moment in time for the Lemont community. Prints are available at the Lemont Area Historical Society.

This 1972 aerial photograph of downtown Lemont was taken during the village's Keepataw Days. The growth over the past 50 years is evident. Some buildings are gone, and other landmarks have not yet been built. The Illinois and Michigan Canal is overgrown, with homes still lining its north bank. Restoring and celebrating the canal has been a major effort of the Village of Lemont and others.

Riders on horseback in Western wear show off the cowboy spirit of Keepataw Days in the 1950s. First celebrated in 1949, the Labor Day festival is named in honor of local Potawatomi Chief Keepataw. A carnival is set up behind them on Main Street. The popular Keepataw Parade would first step off in 1953.

Local businesses and organizations entertain Lemonters as the Keepataw Parade proceeds down Illinois Street in 1955. A decorated work truck from Nelson's Hatchery, once located at 101 Stephen Street, makes the turn at left. The Singer-Warner Mothers' Club, begun in 1948, rides in a float ahead of them, celebrating the "Family Outing of Yester Year." Virginia Reed Park is named in honor of their founder.

The Lemont Jaycees were founded in 1955 as an organization of young men dedicated to the development of their community. They eventually took over the organization of Keepataw Days in the 1960s. While the parade route has changed over the years, one thing remains: Lemonters are enthusiastic to participate in local parades!

Lemont's ethnic groups were regular participants in Keepataw Parades, with Polish, German, and Lithuanian social and religious groups that served the community marching. In this 1979 photograph, members of the Chicago Stock Yard Kilty Band represent Lemont's Irish community. The band continues to make appearances in various parades to this day.

Devastating tornadoes have struck twice in Lemont's history. June 13, 1976, saw the first of the powerful tornadoes, causing a half million dollars' worth of damage, destroying 87 homes, damaging 82 more, and taking the lives of three residents. Nearly every home in this aerial photograph was destroyed. McCarthy Road cuts across diagonally.

Lucya Kromray's severely damaged home is pictured following the 1976 tornado. This storm reportedly traveled 10 miles, produced winds exceeding 200 miles per hour, and lasted over an hour. Tornadoes typically travel around 25 miles per hour, but this one moved at less than half that speed, resulting in severe destruction throughout Lemont. Following its aftermath, homeowners in this area petitioned to be incorporated within Lemont.

On October 15, 1975, the Bicentennial Commission and Lemont Area Historical Society dedicated a new mural, *The Stonecutters*, by famed artist Caryl Yasko on the east wall of 316 Canal Street, now Budnik Plaza. Yasko cofounded the Chicago Mural Group, and her work was featured throughout the Midwest. This mural emphasizes the spirit of those who labored in Lemont's quarries, including women lifting a heavy slab of limestone in honor of Lemont's heroic women.

Since its original creation, Yasko, seen here in 1984, has returned several times to update the mural due to sun fading. In each of her return appearances, she has added new elements. Her most recent visit included a team comprised of Harrison Halaska, Ingrid Kallick, and Rob Moriarty, rededicated on October 8, 2021.

Older Lemonters will recall the narrow bridge over the Illinois and Michigan Canal on State Street before the construction of the current high bridge. This lost view, taken from the base of the old bridge, features the steep road uphill toward St. Alphonsus, as cars cross the Chicago & Alton Railroad and Main Street.

The Lemont Road High Rise Bridge can be seen here, shortly after the start of construction in 1981. Stephen Street Bridge would soon be closed, due to concerns of village officials. The construction of this bridge resulted in the demolition of some historic structures on Main Street and elsewhere but provided safer transportation for residents heading to DuPage County or Interstate 55.

The Lemont Road High Rise Bridge quickly transported residents and visitors to and from DuPage County, Interstate 55, and other destinations, but it bypassed local businesses. There is a lot to be learned in this image. One can see how vital an artery Stephen Street was, traveling under the Santa Fe Railroad, across the Chicago Sanitary and Ship Canal on its old bobtail swing bridge, and then across the Des Plaines River to Lemont Road. The shift in town platting is also apparent: old downtown Lemont stands in contrast to the wooded residential districts on the bluff, with downtown oriented toward the canals and railroads while the residential areas are oriented in cardinal directions. While this bridge diverted traffic past Lemont's historic core, the resurgence in local business and walkable communities has made downtown Lemont a prosperous business district.

Aside from some changed business names, including the Strand, Phillips 66, and Blesch and Welter Hardware, as well as the dated automobiles, this photograph of Stephen Street in downtown Lemont could have been taken today, with some buildings nearly identical to their current appearance. The Lemont Downtown Commercial District was listed in the National Register of Historic Places on September 6, 2016.

In 1973, a chemical spill at Steelco east of downtown Lemont fogged up much of the business district. In this photograph taken by Walter Tedens, Old Central School at the top of the hill is barely visible. Lemont Inn can still be seen at the southwest corner of Stephen and Main Streets. Tedens's photographs were used as evidence in the ensuing trial regarding the spill.

Businesses of the recent past are seen here along Limestone Row on the east side of Stephen Street. Blocks like this one held many memorable shops, saloons, and organizations over the years, each with their own story. This photograph captures the Strand, Hayes & Sons, the Christmas Tree Inn, the Cookie Jar Museum (and soon Brandt Cellars), and Polonia (which lived on as Old Town).

Tom's Place, appearing nearly identical to its present appearance, is seen here in the early 1980s. Lemont residents have been coming to Tom's since 1924. The neon Blatz sign luring residents in has been a staple of Stephen Street. The bar moved from across the street into this location in 1949. A barber's pole can be seen on the left side of the building.

There has been a saloon on this block of Main Street since the Smokey Row days. Nick's Tavern has been a Lemont institution since 1945, and it still serves the Nickburger. Lange's has been downtown since 1983. The building to the left has been lost, but the Wolter's Building (right) has been lovingly restored, as has Nick's, the renovations improving not only the buildings but the appearance of downtown Lemont.

Canal Street may have been the epicenter for Smokey Row, but the standout building is the T.F. Friedley Hardware Store at 311 Canal Street, with its ornamental cast-iron storefront. Built in 1879, its tall parapet is a confectionary mix of architectural ornament unique in Lemont. Most of the buildings on this block have been restored since this photograph from 1989.

Here is a reminder of the ways the automobile transformed downtown Lemont, in this case with the Willys-Knight Building, built about 1925. The brick-and-stone building demonstrates a modern approach to historic styles, with large windows to lure customers into the showroom on 44 Stephen Street. Goodyear tires and auto repair were offered in the rear garage. Ed James was the last dealership in Lemont.

This building once epitomized the changes in transportation. Wagner Brothers built its livery here in 1894, opposite the Chicago & Alton Railroad depot. John Wagner would partner with Joseph Brandt, who later became sole owner. It was sold in 1919 as the automobile replaced horse-drawn carriages. D&M Motors opened here in 1922, selling several makes until becoming a Ford dealer in 1932. Glenn McAdam would buy out his partner in 1934.

Lemont's United Methodist Church at 25 West Custer Street traces its roots to the earlier Methodist Episcopal congregation on Lemont Street, now the Old Stone Church. This stunning Modernist church is tucked away on Singer Hill. The bold form is wrapped with a cedar-shingled exterior and overlooks the former Brown estate and the river valley. Classrooms and a preschool beneath the sanctuary are tucked into the hill.

The old quarries east of downtown were Lemont's secret for decades, where locals enjoyed themselves in all seasons, like in this photograph of skaters from 1979. The Lemont Heritage Quarries recreation area was formally dedicated in 2004. It features hundreds of acres of open space, miles of hiking and biking trails looping around quarries, and fishing. Since 2020, it has been home to an adventure park, The Forge: Lemont Quarries.

A tugboat and towboat dock is located under Lemont Road. A common scene on a working canal, they hide an important industry innovation, a retractable pilothouse. As barges got larger, the captain needed to be higher. But in Lemont, the old Santa Fe Railroad Bridge, built to be moveable, has stood stubbornly still at 19.7 feet over the waterway, requiring barges to be ferried by more adaptable craft.

A second tornado hit Lemont on March 27, 1991. The twister's path veered through Singer Hill along Pieffer and Warner Avenues, State Street, and the Blue Hill area. It hit McCarthy Pointe and then Franciscan Village. Continuing east, it lifted the roof off St. James at Sag Bridge. Fifteen homes were destroyed, and 180 were damaged.

The federal act that created the Illinois and Michigan Canal National Heritage Corridor—the first of its kind—is presented by the Canal Corridor Association to Lew Schmidt, township supervisor; village president Herbert Zielke; and Sonia Kallick of the Lemont Area Historical Society. The heritage corridor act created a new kind of national park, without public lands, where volunteers and agencies work together.

The Lemont Area Historical Society Museum was dedicated on September 17, 1972. Since then, the museum has been visited by thousands of people from all corners of the world. Volunteers conduct guided tours of the museum and lead walking tours of Lemont's landmark buildings and quarries. Continuing efforts are being made to renovate the Old Stone Church and museum. (Courtesy of Molly Hebda Photography.)

The historical society celebrated the 150th anniversary of the I&M Canal's ground breaking with this fun float at the 1986 Keepataw Parade. Since its inception, the LAHS has been an advocate for the canal. The Village of Lemont purchased the I&M Canal from the state in 1970, providing recreational opportunities. In 1995, the two-mile hiking trail along the old canal towpath was dedicated by the village.

Members of the Lemont Area Historical Society hold their banner at the October 1984 dedication of the Lemont Road High Rise Bridge. The LAHS was formed in response to a potential demolition of the Old Stone Church. Since their inception in 1970, the society has been a powerful voice for the community, working to "Save the Valley" and "Save Our School," plus listing several properties in the National Register of Historic Places.

BIBLIOGRAPHY

Andreas, A.T. *History of Cook County, Illinois: From the Earliest Period to the Present Time.* Chicago, IL: A.T. Andreas, 1884.

Buschman, Barbara A., and Rose Yates, ed. *Lemont: 125th Anniversary Edition, 1873–1998.* Lemont, IL: Village of Lemont, 1998.

Cahan, Richard, and Michael Williams. *The Lost Panoramas: When Chicago Changed its River and the Land Beyond.* Chicago, IL: CityFiles Press, 2011.

Camalliere, Pat, and Kay Manning, eds. *History & Anecdotes of Lemont, Illinois, 6th Edition.* Lemont, IL: Lemont Area Historical Society, 2016.

Illinois Department of Transportation, Karen Poulson. *Historic Documentation Record, Western Stone Company (Keepataw Site).* Chicago, IL: Archaeological Research Inc.

Kallick, Sonia Aamot. *Lemont and Its People, 1673–1910.* Louisville, KY: Chicago Spectrum Press, 1998.

———. *National Register of Historic Places Nomination: Lemont Central Grade School.* Lemont, IL: Save Our School, Lemont Historical Society, 1974.

Lanyon, Richard. *Building the Canal to Save Chicago.* Bloomington, IN: Xlibris Corporation, 2012.

Lemont Historic Preservation Commission, Granacki Historic Consultants. Architectural Resources in the Lemont Historic District. 2006.

Michael, Vincent L., and Deborah J. Slanton, eds. *Joliet-Lemont Limestone: Preservation of an Historic Building Material.* Chicago, IL: Landmarks Preservation Council of Illinois, 1988.

Morsicato, Joanna Bossert, ed. *The Illinois and Michigan Canal, Compiled by Edward O. Bossert.* Self-published, 1993.

Thornton, Nancy. *National Register of Historic Places Nomination: Lemont Methodist Episcopal Church.* Lemont, IL: Lemont Area Historical Society, 1986.

———. *National Register of Historic Places Nomination: St. James (Sag) Catholic Church and Cemetery.* Lemont, IL: Lemont Area Historical Society, 1984.

Will County Land Use Department, Wiss, Janney, Elstner Associates Inc. *Rural Historic Structure Survey of Homer Township, Will County, Illinois.* 2002.

Willcockson, Tom. *Passage to Chicago: A Journey on the Illinois & Michigan Canal in the Year 1860.* LaSalle, IL: Canal Corridor Association, 2016.

About the Lemont Area Historical Society

The Lemont Area Historical Society is in the Old Stone Church at 306 Lemont Street, built by the Methodist Episcopal congregation in Lemont in 1861. Listed in the National Register of Historic Places and located in Lemont's historic district, the home of the LAHS contains a rich collection of historical artifacts from Lemont and the surrounding area, exhibited in its history museum.

The purpose of the Lemont Area Historical Society is to preserve the heritage and folklore of Lemont and to operate the museum as a repository for memorabilia and artifacts. Founded in 1970 to save the Old Stone Church, the historical society is a not-for-profit organization that exists through the support of its members. Thank you to all who already support the historical society and museum. Others, we invite you to join. Visit lemonthistory.org to learn more.

DISCOVER THOUSANDS OF LOCAL HISTORY BOOKS FEATURING MILLIONS OF VINTAGE IMAGES

Arcadia Publishing, the leading local history publisher in the United States, is committed to making history accessible and meaningful through publishing books that celebrate and preserve the heritage of America's people and places.

Find more books like this at
www.arcadiapublishing.com

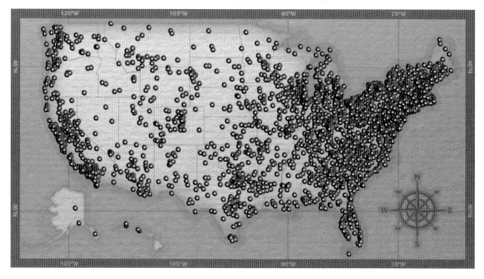

Search for your hometown history, your old stomping grounds, and even your favorite sports team.